Pieces of Me

Rhi Vautrin

BookLeaf Publishing

India | USA | UK

Presentation by *BookLeaf Publishing*

Web: www.bookleafpub.com

E-mail: info@bookleafpub.com

ISBN: 978-93-5744-783-6

First edition 2022

DEDICATION

To my mother.

Finally, something I made that you get to see.

ACKNOWLEDGEMENT

A huge thanks to Nikko, Kiara, Ofilya, Mel, and Cinder. Thank you all for being my sounding boards and thank you for always being amazing. You are some of my biggest inspiration.

And to all the rest of my friends - there are far too many of you to list - all of whom I want to thank personally. You guys keep me sane, and I love each and every one of you. Please forgive me for not typing out all your names.

Not All Men

"Not all Men."
It's a sentence that gets thrown around,
When we talk about the abuse we survive.
It's the cold, invalidating truth in their eyes,
It's "How can you be scared when it's only one
guy?"

"Not all Men."
It climbs up the walls of our subconscious,
When we try to come forward and tell our truth.
It's pushing us down, keeping us reduced.
Ensure we stay in place so they can seduce.

"Not all Men"
It's not the only line in their arsenal,
The things they throw around to hide us away.
To keep us small, and to make us obey,
But it's oh so far from the only invalidating way.

"Not all Men."
Is true to the extent that;

"Not all Men"
Will follow you down a shadowed road.

"Not all Men"
Will be the reason we can't walk alone.

"Not all Men"
Will coerce the answer they want out of you.

"Not all Men"
Will be the reason we hide,
Will be the thing that goes bump in the night,
Will be the thing that causes our greatest fears.

But the men who say that are part of the
problem.
They are the ones who turn their backs.

These good men you bring up,
Are the ones who listen.
Are the ones who uplift our voices.
Are the ones who will believe us.

Because "Not all Men"
Do the things we fear,
When at the party all alone.
When we walk down the street pretending on
our phone,
That cause slide fear down every single bone.

So "Not all Men"
Are the reason we are unsure.

But "Not all Men"
Are good and kind and pure.

"Not all Men"
But it's those men.
Who say these line to make us voiceless.
They are the ones that turn us choiceless,
They are the ones who set out to use and exploit
us.

"Not all Men"
But it's those men
Who bring up others who face out issues
But who do it just so that we don't continue
And care not for the men who share within out
shoes

And it's not to say
That those men don't matter
Or that it doesn't hurt to see their hearts in tatters
But people only bring them up to stop our
chatter.

And it hurts to see
When aside gets brushed those who are culpable
Because talk of what happens makes people
uncomfortable.
When it leave these people feeling themselves
unlovable.

So yes.

"Not all Men"
Is a sentence that gets thrown around,
When we talk about the abuse we survive.
It's the cold, invalidating truth in their eyes,
It's "How can you be scared when it's only one
guy?"

And it is the truth of the words.
That good men exist out in the world.

But when you say these words to invalidate our
trauma.

To make us seem like we are just creating
drama.

Then it is you who we watch for late at night,
It is you who we arm ourselves for, prepared to
fight.
It is you who cause our groups so tight.
It is you, the men who cause fear of our life.

So "Not all Men"
Are cause for terror and tears,
But not all women
Can just move on from our fears.

Injustice

Injustice
Please fill the following form

Some days it makes me
Circle all that apply:
        Sad Angry Numb

That feeling makes me
Circle all that apply:
        Cry Scream Aphithetic

It never makes me
Circle all that apply:
        Happy Excited Giddy

Stawberries and Sunlight

Some days I wonder what it's like
To be made of strawberries and sunlight
The way she is
With her smile of sugar and fiz

Some days I wonder how it feels
To take comfort in knowing I am real
The way she does
Dancing in the rain and sweet air in her lungs

Some days I wish to be she
To be free
To be her
To be me

One day I want to be strawberries and sunlight

Frogs and Clouds

He spends his days
Kissing frogs trying to make princes
Wanting to create a life
Of soft love and white picket fences

He spends his days
Chasing clouds to dance in the rain
Wanting to create a life
Of soft days free of his pain

It was but fate who gave the nudge
To let the clouds bring rain
And rain brings frogs
To give them the life they love

She

She smiles and it lights up the room
She is a jewel
She sounds like a big happy boom

She is ambitious as she is fearless
She is silver
She is the commotion in the motionless

She sings and the songbirds stop
She is moonlight
She causes happiness spinning like a top

But now rooms are dim
And there's no more boom

But now there are flinches
And stillness reigns

But now you hear the bird
And happiness toppled

So tell me why it was you felt the right
To scuff her jewel
To dull her silver

To block her moonlight
Hold her down when she tried to fight

You left her feeling broken
Used
Scarred
Afraid of her own shadow

Who gave you the right
To scare her so deeply

Who gave you the right?

Wait

Tik

Tok

Tik

Tok

There is a stillness in fear
In waiting for results
An answer to your prayers

Tik

Tok

Tik

Tok

There is a fear in stillness
The moment before the results
The limbo you live in

Tik

Tok

Tik

Tok

Tik

Distance

Distance

What a pain

I just want to hug
you

You're still my best friend though

Crazy

Am I crazy?

Does liking her make me wrong
Does it make me evil and bad
Does it take away my ability to be around

Am I crazy?

For not understanding that some love
Runs deeper than others
For loving everyone so unconditionally

Am I crazy?

For finding you and stopping short
Not quite reaching into that void
For not making that leap

Am I crazy?

Am I truly crazy?

Or do you and I just not think the same?

You

You
The single most important thing
That I have ever had the pleasure of having

You
A shot of sugar on for my brain
A part in the clouds on a day full of rain

I know not what I could have done
To deserve the sweet sounds of loving you

Forest Door

They say there is a door in the forest
Who can grant you everything you want
But despite searching and searching
No one seems to find it

But I know the truth

The doorway lives to grant wishes
Not for anything you ever wanted
But instead for those who need to run
Those who hide from all manner of man made
monster

I know the truth

Because I hold the key to this door
I plucked up the roots
I dug out the lake
I put my soul into this haven

I know the truth

Because I am the truth

I Don't Remember

I don't remember my childhood
I hear story of escapades
Things I did that I don't know
Memories that I have no access too

I don't remember much of school
None of the taunts from kids
No memories of the lonely recesses
And the few too many friends

And it hurts because I know
I know it keeps me safe
That I had not a bad childhood
But that in no way means good

It's hard on an 8 year old
To be a social reject
When the word has no real meaning
And you are left on your own to read

It's hard on a 10 year old
To have no real clue
As to who is friend and who is foe
A fear of pity pushes everyone away

It's hard on a 14 year old
To realize that maybe you can have friends
But not to know how
Because you never got to learn

And it's true, I learned
But I learned late
Cues are still missed
Unsure of where to push and pull

I don't remember much of my childhood
I don't remember life on the playground
I don't remember nights spent reading
I don't remember being a child

I don't remember happy
Before happy was a choice I made

Silvered Light

I live my life in a world of bright gold
And what a sight it is to behold

Every colour saturated
Children yelling with joy
A world on the constant move
Every piece exaggerated

But at night I move through silver light
Bathing the world in grey and black and white

A careful stillness
A peaceful serenity
No fight to make
Just sweet moments between us

I Still Love You

Would you hold it against me
If I told you I still love you
That every beat of your heart makes me smile
That every breath of your lungs gives me hope

Because despite what you think
You are perfect to me

But I won't say
Because the world of pain without your love
Is better still
Than the world of pain without you at all

Attic

The door swing open
Bringing with it a flash of light
Memories of a better time
Of warmth and of life
Filter through my brain - frozen

I see the days of my life
When this attic was free of dust
Used for more than storing holiday cheer
Used instead for make believe
When life was simple - free of strife

I see all and nothing
Stuck here in this eternal hell
In this eternal heaven
Watching families live their life
I am stuck - wishing I was something

And soon enough the door closes again
And I am left back to my dark
Watching dust bunnies form
Wishing I were anywhere
Listening to nothing - living life of pretend

Stuck

I watch over and over and over
As seconds turn to minutes
Minutes turn to hours
Hours turn to days
Days turn to weeks
Weeks turn to months
Months turn to years
Years turn to decade
Decades turn centuries

Then I watch as it's jumbled
Hours turn to centuries
Centuries turn to months
Months to seconds
Seconds turn to decades
Decades to weeks
Weeks turn to years
Years turn to hours

Nothing makes sense

I've watched the world begin and end
I've seen humanity collapse

Then I watched it be born

I've spend forever and never
Trapped in time
Unable to change anything
Wishing to do something

I've seen the end
And I will see it again

And there is comfort in the certainty of that one
thing.

Phones

They call us obsessed
Glued to out phones
As if that's such a bad thing

I have the world at my fingertips
Friends I carry in my pocket
A million things I'd never have learned

Obsession can be dangerous
But obsession if different than understanding
What exactly that information means

Not Made To Last

You and I are perfect
We compliment each other like purple and green
Perfect peas in a pod of perfection

You and I are perfect
We laugh at the same jokes no matter how lame
Twin funny bones in a body of laughter

You and I are perfect
We love and love and love until there is no more
to give
Until the times have run out and we love more

But you and I know what comes next

You and I aren't made to last
We love and love
Laugh and laugh
Compliment and match

But we are not each others forever
And it hurts to say
But we can feel the end

And we love each other enough
Just enough to see the end
And leave while there is still love to give

You and I are perfect
We are meant to be
But we aren't made to last

Deep Sea's Monster

There is a creature
Who lives deep in the sea
She is kind
She is scared

There is a creature
Who lives deep in the sea
He chases her
He hunts her

There is a creature
Who lives deep in the sea
She is told she's wrong
She is told she's a monster

There is a creature
Who lives deep in the sea
She begins to believe
She believes she is wrong

There is a creature
Who lives deep in the sea
She is the sea
She is the monster

There is a creature
Who lives deep in the sea
Who listened to him
Who is the dark sea's monster

There is a monster
Who belongs to the dark sea
Who learned to protect herself
Who is on the hunt

Smile

Instructions: Smile
Reason: RBF
Quote: "Come on baby, smile for me"

Lift corners of mouth
Show edge of teeth
Giggle
Light up eyes

Note: Mean it

Boys like nice girls

Don't be rude.

Scream

One day I will yell so loud
The world will feel my pain
And then they shall know

A Single Star
Among The Sky

Sometimes I wander at night
Staring at the sky in wonder
Asking myself what it would be like to be them.
To be a thing of wonder and beauty

I try with all my might to be them.
To use makeup, and highlighter, and sparkles,
All in an effort to make myself shine
But it's never enough

And it's not to say that I don't feel pretty
These things make my skin settle and calm
But they lack the quality to make me shine
To make me a thing of breathtaking wonder

At some point I had accepted this
That I would be pretty
But I would never be the stars and moon
Until I took a closer look

Until I saw the look in my eyes
When excitement filled their view

And suddenly there were stars
Traveling across my body like fireworks

Until I saw the way that the pattern in our eyes
Mimicked that of nebulas light-years away
And I realized that these grays and blues
Formed the stars that I loved so dearly

Until I saw the way that our cells are born
The way they grow as stars die
Splitting apart in a dance
That creates galaxies and life

Until I saw photos of our brain cells
And saw the way they stretched into the
universe
Bridging pathways of life
Holding within us the secrets we want to know

I spent my life thinking I would never be
breathtaking

But I now know differently

I know now that I am the galaxy

I hold stars in my eyes

And life in my cells

And I know now that the universe made me in
her beauty

And I know she smiles as I realize that we are
one in the same.